C000136858

# A VI
# DICTIONARY

# A VERY SWEARY DICTIONARY

From abso-f**king-lutely
to w**kstain: an essential,
if somewhat impolite, style guide

Kia Thomas

A VERY SWEARY
DICTIONARY
by Kia Thomas

First edition published 2020

Copyright © Kia Thomas 2020

Cover design by Elizabeth Grey
Interior design by Eleanor Abraham
Edited by Katherine Trail of KT Editing

Typeset in Bodoni URW and Traveling Typewriter

ISBN: 978-1-8382264-0-4

www.kiathomasediting.com

# Introduction

**WARNING: This book
contains strong language.**

It would be a pretty shite dictionary of swearing if it didn't.

This is not really, though, what you might call a proper dictionary. I hope it will be a useful resource for some people, but I'm not a lexicographer or a linguist. I'm just a copyeditor who really likes swearing.

This book came about because I somehow got a reputation in copyediting circles for being pretty sweary. This is mostly my clients' fault, because they're sweary. Thus I had to become an expert in making style choices regarding swearing, because not all of the swear words my clients use are in dictionaries, often because they've invented them themselves.

So this, really, is less of a sweary dictionary and more of a sweary style guide. But a dictionary sounds less geeky, so that's what it's called. It's not meant to be an exhaustive list of every swear word in existence, but a set of guidelines you could (you don't have to; I'm not the boss of you) follow should you need to decide how to style swear words (in particular compound ones, as they're the ones for which these decisions usually have to be made). Or, if you're not in the writing or copyediting game, perhaps it's just a fun way to recreate the joy of discovering the naughty words in the school dictionary.

# On editing swearing

If you are one of those people reading this for shits and giggles, you can skip this bit. My editing colleagues using this as a resource probably shouldn't.

Swearing can be funny and silly and give us all a good giggle. I'm not going to deny that even after a few years of editing, I still get a bit of a kick out of this kind of shit being my actual job. But swear words are still words. Our clients write them, therefore we owe it to them to treat those words with as much respect as we do the other, non-vulgar ones, and that means checking them carefully for consistency, correctness and appropriateness.

The style choices in this guide are my own

personal ones. Many of the choices follow my preferred dictionaries and style guides, but at times I depart from those authorities. I don't always enforce the choices in this guide if the client has made a different one consistently, unless usage is so generally established that a different style looks like an error (I'm not sure I'd allow "dick-head", for example, unless a character had an actual dick for a head). If you don't agree with my choices, don't follow them. Nobody died and put me in charge of swearing. (Question: who *would* have to die in order for me to be in charge of swearing? Just wondering.)

# International and historical swearing

I am from the UK, so this guide is written in UK English and deals mainly with the style choices I would make in UK English, but I also frequently work in US English, so I make mention of that too. I've left other varieties of English alone as I'd more than likely get too much wrong.

Styling differs little between US and UK English (the main difference being that the former tends to move from open/hyphenated to closed more quickly than the latter does), but the subtleties of local usage are not so simple. For example, a drunk person in the UK can be "fucked" or "pissed" (among many,

many, many other terms), but those words don't have that meaning in the US. It's important to get this right, in fiction especially, because swearing is often used for emphasis, at a time of particular emotion, or for characterisation – all of which are occasions that call for authenticity. A Texas cowboy exclaiming "Oh, buggering bollocks" or a Yorkshirewoman calling someone a "goddamn douche" are likely to draw a reader out of a story and undermine trust in the author.

Take care also when dealing with historical swearing – many terms are far younger, or indeed far older, than you might expect. The *Oxford English Dictionary (OED)* and the website *Green's Dictionary of Slang* are invaluable resources in this respect. For a contemporary audience, it is better to style words in the way the reader would expect than the way they would have been styled in the period in question. For example, if editing a novel set in the interwar period, feel free to use "motherfucker" rather than follow the styling of the word's first entry in the *OED* in 1918, "Mother Fucker".

# On not swearing

In fiction, censoring swearing is not usually something you have to worry about – either swear, if it's appropriate for the character and the audience, or don't. And in other contexts, I'm generally of the opinion that if the material is only likely to be read by adults who have chosen to read that publication knowing it is intended for an adult audience – a book, a blog post, an article in a magazine or newspaper – blanking out part of a swear word seems unnecessarily prissy. But sometimes, for decency's sake, the situation requires it.

Many publications will have a house style on this. However, if you are the person who has to decide how to blank out a swear word, you have a couple of options, depending on your preference and/or which style guide you would normally defer to:

- Spaced en-rules or asterisks, one for each letter (*New Hart's Rules*). As you can probably tell from the cover of this book, asterisks are my preferred option.
- One 2-em rule to represent all the missing letters (*Chicago Manual of Style*).
- Hyphens, one for each letter.
- One ellipsis to represent all missing letters.
- A "grawlix", the string of characters (e.g. @#$%&!) often used to represent a swear word in things like comics. The grawlix has a more comedic effect, so it might not be appropriate in all contexts. And "grawlix" is one of my favourite words ever, but that's not really important.

Whichever option you're using, make sure

13

the meaning is as clear as it needs to be. If it's important that the reader knows which exact word is being used, make sure they have enough information to be able to decode it – is "b—" "bastard", "bitch", "bollocks", or "bugger"? Who can say? Even "b*****d" for "bastard" could read as "buggered" to anyone not counting the asterisks. If context doesn't make it clear, you'll have to do it yourself (by revealing more letters, but you figured that out, right?).

# General
# principles

Here are the general principles I go by when it comes to styling compound swear words, which are largely what this guide is concerned with.

## Close it up when you can

Because usage of hyphens in English is decreasing, hyphenating a swear can look prissy and old-fashioned, and that might not be the effect you're going for (or it might, if it suits the tone of the work). Very often, you're squishing swear words together to make a new word, probably one to insult someone, so you want that comic, Roald Dahl-ish effect, where the new word flows smoothly. (Although I'm pretty sure Roald Dahl never included "thundercunt" in any of his books.) And especially if you are forming a compound noun by combining an obscenity with an object, such as an animal or item of food, it should be one word.

## Leave it open or hyphenate if it looks weird

Highly technical criteria right there. Some words squished together just look a bit odd and can be hard to read (see "ball-ache"). Making things easier on the reader is never wrong.

## Hyphenate for clarity

Some verbs could be misread if left open (see "shit-stirring"). And it's probably unlikely, but there could be times when you need to differentiate between a sweary compound's usual meaning and its more literal meaning (see "cocksucker").

## Normal rules apply for compound modifiers

Follow your usual style guide for compound modifiers (hyphenated before a noun, and generally open after if you're following *Chicago Manual of Style*, or hyphenated if they're formed with a participle if you're following *New Hart's Rules*).

## Don't overthink

Weigh up how much time you're spending on one word against the importance of getting it "right". It's probably not that important. It's easy to agonise over any style choice, but if you're dealing with swear words, especially ones that aren't in a dictionary, chances are you're not editing the type of material where absolute formal accuracy and correctness are paramount. So pick a way of styling it, and stick to it. Consistency is key.

# The Dictionary

# abso-fucking-lutely

*Absolutely, but with a "fucking"
in the middle for emphasis.*

Inserting a word into a compound word
is called tmesis, which is a fun word, and
sweary tmesis is obviously even more fun.
Also fun is expletive infixation, which
sounds really posh but is actually the
insertion of a swear word into a word that
is not a compound, such as "absolutely".

Hyphenate expletive infixation for ease of reading, and sometimes it's wise to tweak a spelling to follow pronunciation, e.g. "Christ all-fucking-mighty".

For tmesis, use your judgement – over-hyphenating can look fussy, so if the word separates easily into its component parts, as is the case in something like "everything", you can leave every fucking thing open.

# apeshit

*A state of high excitement or vexation.*

Animal-shit compounds should be closed for adjectival use. For actual animal faeces, I'd suggest sticking with two words.

# arse over tit

*A less polite version of "head over heels".*

As in "I fell arse over tit down the stairs".

Open, but I could see it being used as a hyphenated compound adjective, for example, "Boris Johnson looks like some kind of arse-over-tit pigeon".

# arsewipe

*An awful person.*

As in "He's an absolute arsewipe". The
US equivalent is, of course "asswipe".

Both closed, but I daresay I wouldn't
object to a hyphen in the US version on
"looks weird" grounds.

# -ass

*Intensifier.*

As in "big-ass clown feet". More common in US English than UK, maybe because "-arse" doesn't quite have the same effect.

Always hyphenate for clarity – "big 'ass clown' feet" just raises all sorts of questions.

# ball-ache

*Something that is tiresome
or troublesome.*

Hyphenated. You could certainly close
it, but in my opinion "ballache" looks
like something you'd find on *Masterchef*:
"I've made a ballache of venison with a
kumquat foam."

# batshit

*Exceedingly irrational,*
*excited or angry.*

Closed, as per apeshit.

# bellend

*General insult.*

I defer to Oxford Dictionaries here and
close it, but it's seen frequently enough
with a hyphen that I doubt anyone could
call it incorrect.

# blowjob

*Oral sex performed on a penis.*

Although not technically, I suppose, swearing, this comes up (fnarr fnarr) often enough that I think it warrants inclusion.

Many dictionaries have this, and the similar "handjob", open, but in the words of Benjamin Dreyer, copy chief at Random House and author of *Dreyer's English*, "it's long since time for blowjobs and handjobs." Quite.

# bullshit

*Something that is
untrue or nonsense.*

Although this, unlike "batshit" and
"apeshit", is usually used a noun, I'd
still close it up when used figuratively.
Should you have cause to talk about
actual shit from an actual bull, you
might leave it open to avoid confusion.

# clusterfuck

*An extremely
messy situation.*

Closed. One of my favourite words,
although obviously not so much of a fan
of finding myself in one.

# cock-block

*To prevent someone (usually a man) from succeeding in their attempt to sleep with someone.*

US sources seem to prefer this closed, but sorry, I like the hyphen, and this is my style guide. That's for the verb, by the way. Oxford Dictionaries has an entry for it as a noun, but I'm not sure how frequently people call others "a cock block". But then I don't have one to be blocked.

# cocksucker

*General insult.*

Closed. Perhaps hyphenate if you need to distinguish between someone who is fellating and someone who is not.

# cockwomble

*General insult.*

Closed, as are all cases of a one-syllable swear plus a two-syllable animal: "shitgibbon", "crapweasel", "fuckpigeon".

Should you come across the less typical combination of a two-syllable swear plus a one-syllable animal, I would advise you to exercise your editorial judgement: "horse-bastard" may be easier to read than "horsebastard", whatever one of those might be.

# dickhead

*General insult.*

Closed. Pretty sure no one left on the
planet is still hyphenating it, but you
never know.

# douchebag

*General insult.*

Relatively uncommonly used, although widely understood, in the UK. Closed, as per "shitbag". And the lesser-spotted "turdbag".

# douchecanoe

*General insult.*

Closed. In general, a swear plus an inanimate object = closed compound. Further examples include "fucksticks", "fucknugget", "crapburger"... the possibilities are endless.

You might want to hyphenate for a doubled letter, such as in "shit-tractor". No, I don't know what one of those might be or if anyone might ever use that term, but I'm working on general principles here.

# fuck-a-doodle-doo

*General exclamation.*

Used when running late for four
weddings and a funeral.

Don't forget your hyphens. Unless you're
instructing someone to fuck something
called a "doodle doo". And if you are,
I'm not sure I want to know.

# fuck all

*Absolutely nothing.*

That's the definition of it, by the way;
I'm not giving you words that don't
mean anything.

Generally open, although a hyphen is
helpful in phrases like "fuck-all else".

# fuckboy

*A man with a very casual or disrespectful attitude to women and sex.*

That might not be the best definition, because I think I'm too old and uncool to really know what one is. But I do know it should be closed.

# fuck buddy

*A person with whom one has casual sex on a regular basis.*

Open. And obviously a lowercase "b", unless you're writing some kind of disturbing *Elf* fanfic.

# fucked-up-ness

*The state of being fucked up.*

I prefer two hyphens for clarity, but my editing colleagues are split between this, "fuckedupness", and "fucked-upness", so I'm unwilling to be prescriptive about this – use whichever feels right to you.

We can also throw "fuckedupedness", with or without hyphens, into the mix if you really want a wild time.

# fuckface

*General insult.*

Closed, as are "twatface", "buggerface", "dickface", "cuntface", "bollockface", "shitface", "pissface", "bastardface", "wankface" and other such affectionate names for one's life partner.

# fuck-me

*Indicative of desire to
engage in sexual intercourse.*

Hyphenated as an adjective only, as
in "fuck-me shoes". Open for the
imperative exclamation/invitation. And
obviously, the wearing of anything to
which the adjective could be applied
does not imply the imperative form.

# fuckload

*A lot.*

Closed. Can be singular or plural: "I
have a fuckload of work to do" or "I
have fuckloads of work to do".

# fuck off

*Go away.*

Obviously open as a phrasal verb, but
it is also used as an adjective in some
parts of the world (such as my house),
in which case hyphenate: "There's a big
fuck-off spider over there."

# fuck someone over

*To betray or treat someone unfairly.*

Keep it in that order where possible,
particularly when the "someone" is
an individual rather than a group.
"Fucking over Bob" sounds as though it
requires a harness.

# fuck-ton

*A lot.*

I tend to hyphenate this, to stay
consistent with my preferred styling of
"shit-ton", but many styles leave it open.
Use imperial "ton", unless using the
phrase "metric fuck-tonne", which some
may argue is redundant, but if you can't
be redundant when you're swearing,
when can you be, eh?

# fuck up

*To make a mistake/do something badly.*

If something is "fucked up" it implies something about it has gone wrong in some way.

Open as a verb, and I prefer it hyphenated ("fuck-up") as a noun, although some dictionaries have it as one word ("fuckup").

# fuck you

*An expression of anger or defiance.*

All forms should be open according
to Oxford Dictionaries, but I like to
hyphenate the adjective, in a fuck-you
kind of way.

# fuckwit

*General insult.*

Closed. Do people say this outside the UK? They should.

# goddamn

*General exclamation/intensifier.*

There are many variants of this, none of
which could really be considered wrong
– "goddamned", "goddam", "God
damn", etc. – but this is my preference:
closed, uncapitalised, with the "n" on
the end and no "-ed".

# goddammit

*General exclamation.*

For all I like the "n" in "goddamn", I
find it looks weird in "goddamnit".
Like a goddam nit.

# handjob

*Stimulation of a penis by, unsurprisingly, a hand.*

Closed, as per "blowjob". You don't want space here.

# horseshit

*Something that is
untrue or nonsense.*

Closed, as per "bullshit". Again, leave
open for literal horse poo.

# jack shit

*Absolutely nothing.*

Open, just like its British cousin, "fuck all".

# mindfuck

*Something confusing or disturbing.*

Closed. Trying to figure out how to style
swearwords is sometimes one of these.

# motherfucker

*General insult.*

Closed. Never hyphenate, unless, I suppose, you really need to emphasise that someone had sex with someone's mum.

# pisshead

*A habitually drunk person.*

Closed. Just one of the many, many swearwords the UK has relating to drunkenness.

# piss-poor

*Low quality.*

Hyphenated before the noun, open
after. This is a piss-poor dictionary. This
dictionary is piss poor.

# piss-up

*A social gathering involving
large quantities of alcohol.*

Hyphenated, as in "couldn't organise
one in a brewery". But leave open for
the verb: "Go and piss up a rope".

# prick-tease

*A woman who falsely leads a man to believe she will have sex with him.*

Also "cock-tease".

Hyphenated. Avoid using uncritically, because ugh.

# rat-arsed

*Drunk.*

Hyphenate for another UK drink-related term. Why does one nation need so many ways of describing inebriation? Are we drunk too much?

# shit-fit

*A tantrum.*

Hyphenate. Some dictionaries have it
open, but that makes me think of shoes
that give you blisters. Those are a shit
fit.

# shitbag

*General insult.*

Closed for the insult, open for a bag that
isn't very good, and hyphenated for a
bag in which you carry shit.

# shit-eating

*Smug.*

Hyphenated, as in "a shit-eating grin".
Not used much in the UK. Perhaps we
don't grin enough. Too busy drinking.

# shit-faced

*Drunk.*

My preference is to hyphenate, but the
trend appears to be towards "shitfaced",
particularly in the US. Whatever; I'm
behind the times and I like it.

# shithead

*General insult.*

Closed, same as "dickhead". Do people still call other people "shitheads"? It feels very nineties to me. But then if all that velvet and faded denim can come back, maybe so can this.

# shithole

*An unpleasant place.*

Closed. Important usage note: you may
use this to describe your own hometown,
but woe betide anyone else who does.

# shit-hot

*Very good.*

Keep this hyphenated even after the noun to avoid confusion, e.g. "I am shit-hot at swearing."

# shithouse

*A toilet.*

Closed. "Built like a brick shithouse" is a bloody marvellous phrase, but UK readers may not be familiar with the US definition, which, according to Oxford Dictionaries, is "(of a woman) having a very attractive figure". Which is obviously quite different.

# shitload

*A lot.*

Closed. Just like "fuckload", both
singular and plural forms are used.

# shit-scared

*Terrified.*

Hyphenated at all times, even after a noun. For example, "Copyeditors are shit-scared of publishing anything because readers may have unreasonable expectations of perfection." Without the hyphen, the reader may inadvertently see "Copyeditors are shit." And we all know that ain't true.

# shitshow

*An event or situation that is
chaotic or has gone badly wrong.*

Closed, unless you went to the theatre
and had to watch a ninety-minute
monologue about cement set to a
soundtrack of experimental free jazz.
That would probably be a shit show.

# shit-stirring

*Causing trouble or discord
between two or more parties.*

Hyphenated. Compare "Are you really
that stupid or just shit-stirring?" with
"The sugar's all at the bottom of my tea
thanks to your shit stirring."

# shitstorm

*A whole host of bad stuff.*

Closed. I'm trying to decide if a "shit storm" is one that is pathetic, therefore fails at being a storm, or a strong one, which makes life shit for those who encounter it.

Perhaps a "shit-storm", with a hyphen, might be a storm of literal shit, but I hope that isn't a common enough occurrence to warrant discussion.

# shit-ton

*A lot.*

My preference is to hyphenate, although,
as with "fuck-ton", many prefer it open.
Admittedly the likelihood of confusion
with "a ton that is shit" is small.

Never close it, because "Shitton" is
clearly a small village in England,
somewhere between "Shitton Magma"
and "Shitton-on-the-Wold".

# son of a bitch

*General insult.*

Generally open, but go ahead and use "sonofabitch" if it feels right for the character/voice/situation.

# thundercunt

*General insult.*

Closed, as with other swear-plus-noun combinations. This one gets its own entry just because I like it.

# twat-faced

*Of a person, having an
extremely disagreeable face.*

Hyphenate as a compound adjective to
describe someone or something with
a twatty face, but close if being used
as a synonym for "shitfaced", or for
"twatface" as a noun.

# wankstain

*General insult.*

Closed. As is "jizzstain". And I've never
had cause to call someone a "cumstain"
or a "spunkstain", but what the hell,
let's close those too.

# Resources

A haphazard collection of sweary things I have found useful in creating this guide and in the editing of swearing in general.

My preferred free **dictionaries** are:

For contemporary UK English: Oxford University Press's free English dictionary at lexico.com

For contemporary US English: Merriam Webster's free dictionary at merriam-webster.com

For historical usage, the *Oxford English Dictionary* (oed.com) is a wonderful resource – it is a subscription service, but you may be able to access it for free via your local library membership.

**Media style guides** can be very helpful, as they are often more up-to-date than dictionaries and far less buttoned-up than institutional style guides.

Buzzfeed's style guide (buzzfeed.com/emmyf/ buzzfeed-style-guide) is always on the cutting edge of language use, particularly with regard to internet slang and all things sweary.

**Other online resources:**
*Strong Language* (stronglang.wordpress.com): In the authors' own words, "a sweary blog about swearing". There is nothing I could possibly add to that description, except to say that if you enjoyed this book you should definitely check it out.

*Green's Dictionary of Slang* (greensdictofslang. com): a brilliant free resource that covers far more than swearing, showing centuries' worth of slang terms, including when they were first used. Hours of fun for (maybe not quite) all the family.

# Acknowledgements

This book would not exist without the work, generosity, inspiration, time and filthy mouths of many people:

The team who worked on this book: my editor, Kat Trail; my typesetter, Eleanor Abraham; and my cover designer, Elizabeth Grey.

My amazing friends and colleagues Sarah Dronfield and Jill Cucchi, for reading my drafts and offering endless support.

The editing communities on Twitter, on Facebook, and in the CIEP, for being entertained by my swearing and encouraging me to do more of it, and for generally being really fucking awesome. If I start mentioning people individually I'll both never stop and inevitably miss someone, but please know that I love you all.

My clients Tillie Cole and Elizabeth Grey, North East lasses who know how to swear. But maybe not always how to hyphenate. I owe all my expertise to you two.

I thank you all from the bottom of my sweary little heart.

# About the author

Kia Thomas has been a fiction editor since 2016, and has been swearing for much longer than that. She lives in the north east of England with her husband and two daughters. Her hobbies include yoga, spending too much time on the internet, and telling her children to stop fighting over Minecraft. She is also an extremely unsuccessful author of literary fiction.

Printed in Great Britain
by Amazon